Feelings
From the _Heart_

Feelings
From the *Heart*

Love Poems For Regina

Kevin A. Hickson

To order additional copies of this book, contact:
Xlibris Corporation
1-888-795-4274
www.Xlibris.com
Orders@Xlibris.com
122342

Contents

Dedicated to my wife, my lover,
my muse and soul-mate

My Lover

With my eyes

I love you,

With my words

I love you,

With my mind

I love you

With the deep within

I love you,

With my heart,

I love you.

With all ways

I love you.

Places

Manhasset Bay

The radiant sun
Reflects on the water
In a brilliance
That is the image of
What I see when you
Enter a room.

The gentle breeze
Coming off the bay
Caresses my face
Like the touch of
Your lips
When we kiss.

The sound of the waves
The song of birds
Echo the quiet peace
That fills me
When you say
I love you.

Lifted up I am
From all cares
I am like a buoy
Bobbing up and down
And ringing likes a bell
For all to hear
I love you too.

The Dinosaur Jungle

When my children were young
The trees behind our home
Grew straight and tall
Grew so quickly their trunks
Spindly thin
No resistance given to the wind
The leaves like sails
Captured the air
And pulled their tops to the ground.
So green those leaves
So lush, so tempting
For the passing Apatosaurus
To take a noon time snack
For this was the Dinosaur Jungle.
Oh how the children loved
To make believe.
Yet creatures real existed too.
Owls and pheasants and
Songbirds of all sizes and colors
Filling the air and branches with song

Would stop to cool their wings
And take a drink
Turtles, rabbits, raccoons
Squirrels, quail and an occasional sly fox
Would munch on the garden flowers.
How wonderful to be a child
And see creation so.
Now the children are grown
Gone, gone, gone
The jungle, so many creatures
Real and not
Called home
Passing away
Amid the bustle of new building
And sprawl
Only a few sparrows now remain
To cool themselves
On a summer day
Oh where is that place
Where my children did once live and play.

Tracy's Arm

The quiet still water undisturbed,
Except by the fall of water running down
The steep sides of the ice carved walls,
Rock, now green, but once so white,
Reflects the rising sun.

The water deep and dark reflects
Like a mirror.
In this arm of the sea,
Moving ever so gently
The ever changing guard of azure blue icebergs
Make their way to become part of the sea
Finishing their long journey
From the top of the mountain
Still covered with snow

Stillness, this is a place of quiet.
The stillness broken only
By the splash of a seal
Moving from ice to ice
With her young.

Top of the World

Outside the window
Lies a land so foreign
No so alien it is beyond
My comprehension to believe
Such a place could exist
The ground below
A river of white
Extends as far as the eye can see
Interrupted only by the sharp points
Of mountaintops popping up
Like islets in a sea of white cotton
The clouds on the horizon too
Are indistinguishable from the snow
Save for the gray overcast that separates
The cirrus from the cumulus
This is the most extreme place on earth.
Nothing could live here
Save an ice worm
Yet it is a source of life
The snow, ever moving downward
Eventually to rejoin the sea
The end of a journey
That began at the top of the world.

Aloha

The macadam surface
Flanked by the red dirt,
The remains of iron oxide
Deposited long ago when this isle
Rose from the sea red and hot
Coming from the center of the earth.
Is soon left behind
Giving way to a surface of shells and stone
Crushed by the thousand of times
Travelled by wagons gathering
The cane and taro that still grows here.
Soon the way is flooded
The moisture carried
By the trades a thousand miles
Condense and fall here first
Making the way impassable

For a simple four wheeled transport
Hugging too close to the ground.
So on foot to a place
Just beyond these fields teeming green
Protected by gently rising dunes
Lies a shore long and wide with sand
That barks to announce the steps of those who enter its realm.
To one side standing tall
Rising are the cliffs of Napli
Oh so lush and green
Ahead the Pacific rolls its waves gently to the shore
The sun beams bright
Warm not hot
What a peaceful place
No wonder everyone says..
Aloha!

The Stadium

What awe struck me
That first time,
Coming round the corner from the Concourse
Standing so big, so tall . . .
So gigantic,
I first saw the Stadium.
Crossing under the el
And entering what seemed
Like a tunnel,
Illuminated only by a shaft of light
Coming down from a ramp leading upward
Moving toward this light,
I emerged back into the day
Dumbstruck by a sea of green grass
Like none I had ever seen.
This was the field of dreams.
Here, the heroes of my youth,
Mickey, Bobby, Tommy
Whitey, Roger and Yogi
Not missing a move
In utter amazement, thrilled us.

I come here again
Now older, but still
Filled with the same sense of joy,
With my family,
Regina. Tracy and Matt.
That same grass
Still so green, the perfect background
For the heroes of today
Thrill us in much the same way.
Derek, Tino, Mike
Andy, Mariano, and Paul
Traditions and pride kept alive.
I will be sad to see this go.
Some places are like magic
This place I shall miss.

The Lighthouse

Shining beacon
A guide in a hill
Spreading life-giving light
Upon the shoals and rocks
The Scylla and Charybdis
That pose dangers along our way.
Those who linger on the water
Sailing through the channels
Yearn longingly for the hope
The distant flicker of light
Assuring their journey to be safe
Built firmly with block of stone
And tubes of steel
It withstands
The storms wind and rain
And all the hammerings of nature.
The light continues
Its mission to shine on
Illuminating our way.

Cypress Springs

What a strange, exotic spot
Hot but dry
Water all about
Not really a swamp
And more like a lake
Teeming with tall grass
And all manner of life
Grass gives way to islets and trees
With hanging moss
Dangling from branches
Like eerie ear rings
Making them seem taller.
Cattle graze
Gators laze
A turtle lifts its head
Looks about
Then settles back down
Warming in the midday sun
A blue heron
Stoic like a sentinel on guard
Suddenly in a start
Flaps its wings
And takes flight.

The Windjammer

Across the washed teak planking
The fresh salt air
A welcome breeze
Along with a touch of sea-mist
Cools in relief of the tropic sun
Not a sound made
Moving across the water
The sails filled
The wind jammed against the canvass
Propel from isle to isle port to port
This our home our life our sport
The tightening of the sheets
A halliard slapping against the mast
The waves lapping on the hull
Eight bells, the watch is done
Breaks the peaceful silence
As the ship jives to keep its course
In touch with earth
The feel of nature
Its magnetic force comes alive
Like a current flowing up from the rudder
To hands gripping firm the helm
Heading south south west
A safe harbor where to rest.

My Yard

Oh what a day
My garden it needs care
It cannot wait until May
When the flowers bloom so fair

The ground is hard
Beneath my feet
Around the yard
I'll spread mulch and peat

I must give it time
For the grass to grow
It will all be fine
Unless of course it snows

Spirit of Ninety-Eight

A spirit of a time passed
A different sort of travel
Not so formal, hecticless
More patient, slower
An anachronism now
To see the sea
How a cruise ought to be
Hums of the engine
Water against the bow
Quaint lounge and a small cabin
More like a cottage
More like home
Calls out enjoy what's to come.
Close personal
A mature way to see
Lands still mostly unspoiled
And a chance to sit and talk
With acquaintances' new
Of these trailways we walk
A loss it would be
The small way to pass on
Time will tell can viable remain
A way not grander bigger longer
A style not really free can hang on
To me more of a memory
So others can see how great
To sail on the Spirit of Ninety-Eight.

Great White North

Nature has turned
My world upside down
A blowing whiteness formed
Spreading everywhere flakes like seeds sown
More and more amassing
Like a field of wheat now waist high
Blown by wind 'round swirling
Sounds of howls as if the banshee cries
Slowly steadily covered
All roads, walks and lawns
Until like a land wasted
Travelers express a face forlorn
All colors bow to the might
This blinding white itself shows
Fading all else gray in soft light
Filtered by the falling snow
A vast rippled sea
Like waves coming forth
It breaks before me
The great white north
Surely one can posit
With this bottled storm uncorked
Alaska has come to visit
My home State of New York.

Alaska

Land of the Northern Star
Vast beyond imagination
Beauty hard to comprehend
Contrast, stark colors and gray
Stand in opposition
Glaciers, Grizzlies and birds of prey

The midnight sun in summer
Days without end
Sharply different from winter
When night does days emend
Teasing us to question
Through the ever twilight
Will the sun rise again?

Wilderness untouched
Saved from
Man's intruding desire to develop
Spoiling areas environed
Yet here stemmed
Leaves a beauty without parallel
A nature admired.

A rugged people
Close to earth
Close to sea
A home a place
Created to be free
That seems to us off far
Land of the Northern Star

The Gathering

Around the table
Arrived guests do sit
Waiting patiently to wit
An abundant repast to sample
Sons, Daughters and nephew
Aunts, uncles and nieces
Amid talk and fun cutting pieces
A bit to big to chew
You, I can't understand
Your mouth is too full
Are your speaking of wool
Or what has happened in the land
Oh how amusing, completely
These diners can be
Yes something silly to see
This nutty gathering of family

The Closing

Pile upon piles
Paper, lots of paper
Page upon page
Staples, clips and clamps
Holding it all together
Copies of everything
Birth, death, marriage
Certificated of all kinds
Copies more copies
Deeds, taxes, bills
Buyers, sellers brokers
Bankers, lawyers, agents
All gathered together
Around a table
Signing here, signing there
Everywhere signing
Mortgage, loans, titles
All together set
Done, in place
Checks going
Back and forth
Signed, sealed
It is done.

The Shore

I have come to the sea
Many times
A glimpse of serenity to seize
Like a dream.
Hearing oft the repeated
Crash and splash of a wave
Ever so slowly reducing
Earth and rock to sand
Deposited so long ago
Where mile high ice
Stood this ground
Upon which now
Rest my tired feet.
In time this too
Claimed will be
The relentless approach
The coming of the sea
Taking back for its present form
What it left
But would not let go
Only on loan for today.
This place has a rhythm
My breath now
In tide-tuned beat complies
Takes my spirit aloft
Along with sea-birds winged
Silently soaring
In the moment they whisper
Enjoy.

People

The Apprentice

With eyes alert
All is taken in
Not word said
Yet all is heard
Not a beat missed
Seeing is learning
In every action
A message sent
Deep into memory planted
Ready for some future action
A moment of decision
A moment of reason
A moment of truth
A moment the character formed
Defines not only the apprentice
But the master too.

Reflection on St Agnes of Bohemia

Good King Wenceslaus
We know the song how he looked out
Had a sister Agnes
Endowed with virtue
Like her namesake of Rome
Chaste, pure and sacred
A Poor Clare became
Devoting life to service
The poor, the sick, the needy

His favorite carol
The feast of Stephen
A beggar by a fountain
Named for Agnes
Empowered by the Spirit
The King aids the wandering soul
The Lord in our midst

How is it . . . Why it it..
A thought implanted by a song
Obscure characters from long ago
First heard as a child
Continues at ninety-one
Compelling to compassion
Peace, Joy, Hope and Love . . .
Faith!

Black Shoes and A Red Tie

The black shoes
Not the white ones
With the blue stripes
No, the black ones there
Like the ones daddy has
And a red tie too
Just like this one
These I want mom
I know it's strange
Cause I'm small
But with a shirt of white
And pants tan
I'll be a big boy, tall
Dressed in my black shoes and red tie
Just like daddy

The Trio

Are they on an adventure
Having fun among the sights and sounds
Food smiles and joys
Taking it all in they seem like boys
Larger than life
This is all a blast
It's a song
Like one from days of school
A three part one
Tenor baritone and bass
About life and love
Sung strong with emotion
How great to be together
What a time to remember.

My Three Men

Grandfather, father and son
Thirty plus
Separate three
Years in time
Almost thirty more
Now almost a century
Life divided 'tween three
Grandfather, father and son

Two are fathers
All three are sons
Three of the same spirit
Success through effort
The motto Hickson
They share in fun
So much life to see
So much lived
By one . . . Bee.
Grandfather, father and son

In the middle so busy
Going here going there
Doing things for others
Not stopping

For self to care
Careful though
To take in
What matters most . . . Kevin.
Grandfather, father and son

On the end, youth
The vibrant future
Ready to explore
Brave outdoors
Full of hope, idealistic
Fits you
Eagle Scout . . . Matthew
Grandfather, father and son

Oh fortunate three
Generations of family
To see so much
To listen
To risk
Surely to love
My three men
Grandfather, father and son.

Boy to Man

Where is the boy
Sitting up in bed
Holding his favorite toy
Pulling the cover over his head
Calling out in fright
Hits a mark
What goes bump at night
Hiding in the dark
Suddenly a lamp is lit
There stands by the door
His hero just a bit
Speaking softly and more
Gently calming
Chasing the bad dreams
Sitting until quiet a-lasting
Peace returned it seems

A father makes all safe
As time all to fast
Moves along apace
Passing all is past
Roles can be retold
Age can demand
A father now old
Feels a gentle touch
And lifting up his eyes
Knows he has done much
With great effort tries
Holds his tears to stand
But keeps a quiet joy
Even with a trembling hand
And knows where is the boy
The boy is now the man.

Husky

Are you barking at me?
Are you barking at me?
There you are
Dancing with excitement
As I come through the door
The work day over, energy spent.
Such a smile in your eyes
Dashing all about the room
Suddenly you're down on all fours
Ready to leap up
Giving kisses and more
This must be your favorite thing
For this moment anyway.

Memorial Day

Flags waving
Crowds cheering
Veterans. boy scouts, firemen
Marching. marching
Bands playing Sousa
The Thundered, Semper Fidelis,
The Stars and Stripes forever
All in remembrance
Of those not here
Who still keep guard
On foreign shores forever
Where they fell
Men now old
A poppy stuck in lapels
Tell of comrades
Left behind
Flanders, Italy. the Saar
Small far off islands too
Tarawa. Pelieu and others
Lost now to the present
Yet each time "Old Glory" passes
These tired legs rise
And give salute
The symbol of the bond
Uniting the living and the gone
Freedom

Nature

Uncertainty

There are times
When things seem
So dark
Dark
Like the night
When the moon
Refuses
To show itself.

How insecure
This lack of light
Itself only reflected
Makes us feel
For in our not seeing
We doubt
That the light
Ever existed

What of this
Lack of light
This dark
Do we fear?
We do not see
And thereby
Do not know
What is there
Yet we know it is
For we have
Seen it before

We allow
Our fear
To take hold
Fear . . . or the world
Fear . . . so consuming
Fear . . . so dread
Fear . . . we are alone
Fear . . . we are . . .
Un-loved

Love . . .
We are loved
We are made in love
And so
In trusting this love
There is
Nothing to fear
Love brings us
Courage
Courage that smashes
Our fears
And love lights
A lamp
To burn deep
In our hearts
Chasing the dark away.

A Soft Day

'Tis a soft day
The Spring rain
Neither hot nor cold
Gently moistens the air
As it falls
Delicately on the ground.

The droplets fill
Small puddles
With rings moving outward
Filling the space with motion
As if trying to reach
Back to the sky
From where it fell

But the droplets
Trapped by the movement of the Earth
Slowly seep into the soil
Brings life giving water
To trees grass and plants
To set a thousand flowers to bloom

The rain is like
Your love
So freely given me
And returned
With joy to thee
Giving us life
Renewed
Refreshed
Reborn

Our love blooms
As surly as the flowers will
Just as the rain fills
Their roots
You give me life my dear
And this will be my thoughts
When ever
'Tis a soft day.

The Coming Void

The air gets cool at night
Dusk comes a little sooner each day
The evening sky gets violet
Before turning dark
The void is coming early this year
The beloved game
Played by nine around the diamond
Gives way to the falling leaves of autumn
Sending the boys of summer home for the cold days ahead
Putting away for now the gear
Simply bearing the interlocking NY
Twelve and a hundred days to wait
For a return for the players to train
What a time to wait
This will, with the winter pass
Patience is the order of they day
Before it is felt, the call will be heard
Along with anthems and bands
Tow great words . . . Play Ball!

Metamorphic Love

Soild
Like a rock
The love song goes.
How? How is this possible?
Stones upon the ground
Many kinds
Smooth, rough
Hard to the touch
Lifeless
Not like you or I
Or are they?
Are we rocks?
Do rocks love?
No, we are not rocks.
But we can say
Love rocks us

Love causes change
Without love we are like
Stones lying on the ground
But with love
We are pushed
Pushed back into the earth
Deeper and deeper
Under pressure
Finally melting from the weight above
Changed into something new
United, melded, wed
No longer two, now one
Love rocks us.

Going Deep

Water, steel gray
Reflected from an overcast sky
Water, deep
Carved by ice in time gone by
Water, cold
Almost flat, undisturbed
Water, home
For creatures unperturbed
Water, under
Full of life
Water, source
Of fish and krill
Water, still
Just barely a ripple
Water, a blow
Comes from below
Water, a peek
Whale going deep.

Ice Castle

A castle of ice floating majestically
In the ever still water
Its deep dense blue
Reflected on the surface
Like an image in a mirror.
The serenity of this scene
This castle of ice
This peace is the end
A journey of snow
Fallen high on mountain passes
A thousand years ago.
Here it stands
Aground
Flipped over in the warming late spring waters
Its jagged edges
Giving up the bits of dirt and rock
Scoured from the hillsides
Settle on the bottom.
Melting now, ever faster
Returning the water to the sea.
The cycle continues
As this moisture will condense again
And alight on the mountains
As new fallen snow
But for now
In a few more days
This castle of ice will be no more.

Butterfly On Wheels

On the road
Care on wheels, that's me
Sometimes like a butterfly
Flying here, landing there
Dodging the fools out here,
Which way, which way
North, south, east west
From one place to another
Destination patients.

Do they dream
The chaos driven through
To get here
To see to their needs
To give the RN TLC.
No, I don't think so.
They see only the road ahead
They will go alone
The road that keeps going
One way
Once on it, no going back
Bless them O Lord
Bring them Peace.

Morte du Concorde

The blazing sun shines brightly in the sky
As the moisture comes in from the sea,
Raising the humidity to that level
That makes everything sticky.
Rolling down the lane,
The slick and stylish Concorde
Glides across the dark macadam surface,
Floating, with ease around corners
and purring like a lion,
Its teal green body shines and glistens in the bright day.
Like a statue it is set above the flat road
On alloy wheels that act like pedestals
Raising it off the curb.
It is a design delight.
But Lo!
This hazy, hot and humid day
Has its long talons outreached like a raptor
Ready to snare its prey.

The heat, the years, the miles come together,
The compound fibrous seals that keep the power of this ride in place,
Strain and suddenly
Like a silent bulging aneurism
Give way and its head blows,
Spilling the precious cooling liquids throughout the system
Poisoning the cylinders that for so long
Made it go with chunks of rubber and grease
Being exhaled with the acrid smell of hot metal and anti freeze.
Alas it rolls to a gentle halt,
Stopping,
Never to float along the byways again.
Now Concorde begins it's last journey
Borne away by a snow white flatbed pallbearer.
Yet all is not over for the great machine
Somewhere, like a Phoenix it may arise
Changed into something new
Or making one of its kind whole again
Recycled.

The End of the Trail

Did you ever wonder
What lies at the end of the trail?
Ever so slowly the path leads
Winding and pointing ever forward
Through the forest, trees and plants
Teeming with life and rich colors.
Each step brings something new
The ground at times is soft
From moisture held in the moss
The wind gently moves around
Carrying with it the sound of the nearby river
All around are sign we are not alone,
Scat, says a moose is nearby,
A big footprint with points tells us
A grizzly has come this way.
Better walk softly
Be sure to hang loose.
Moving on it seems as if the hills on each side
Will come together
To scal the end of this valley.
In and out of the canopy we go
More forest, more tundra
Then without warning
The trail just ends.

Vespers

The day is done,
The day is done.
The Sun slowly descends
Calling to all, 'Tis time to rest,
And reflect on this day and
How blessed we are
To be born free.

Freedom,
Freedom
So precious, so dear
Secured by generations
Both past and yet to come.
Lord, continue Your grace
Upon us and this place,
This land
America

Monarch Child

Your orange and black colors
Moving here and there
About the yard
Signal the late afternoon of summer
Soon to be done.

Long weeks hiding
The hot days of July passing
Bundled neath a shroud
Waiting, transforming
So all is new
Soon to take off.

In a paradox
Effort and ease expended
Carried on air
Wings raise and lower
You alit on a flower fair
Taking a rest
Soon to fly on.

The Great One

The great one stands tall
Like a sentinel
Guarding the land
Guiding the river
Reflected in a wonder lake
It is mysterious
Ever hiding its face in the clouds
Always playing peek-a-boo
With those who come to see the two high peaks
One facing north
The other taller still looking south.
No climb is taller
Tough is not enough
To describe as the challenge
Is only for the best and most experienced
Its stature, imposing, declares
"Come, if you dare."
For it stands formed through time unending
By movement for below unseen
And first spoken in Askabaskan
Denali!

Sailing

A graceful scene
Not a sound
Save wind in canvass
Stretched like a drum skin
Moving swiftly
Through the waters
Sleek, soft and trim
Sound only of cutting water
In the background midst
Voices laughing
Enjoying the sun
Reflected off the water
Shimmering like sequins
As this simple lady glides past
The boom let out on a run set
Ready about, a cry
And coming about so
Speed increases and the sleek ship
Heels with a rush of excitement
The port side out of the water
She cuts by at a rakish angle
Racing home.

Sea Dawn

My rest upon the deck
Escaping the hot
Sticky heat below
Is peaceful
Gently rocked by waves
Like a baby in its cradle
Stretched out I see
A multitude of stars
Impossible to count
They lead the way in the dark
Off-setting our silhouette
Against the dark water
Indistinguished from the horizon
They appear like infinity
Far ahead to the east
A faint trace appears
An arc of purple lilac
Like a haze
Backlight the clouds
Signaling soon
A new day

Chilkat Float

Floating, flowing
Moving in a current
Cold icy water
Down from the mountains
Slowly melting snow.

Floating, flowing
A course back and forth
Braided like a pony tail
Weaving in and out
Threading, tying a knot

Floating, flowing
Little bits of gray matter
Built up along the banks
In rain away washed
A new route made

Floating, flowing
The water icy cold
A promise of life
Eagles await
Salmon returning home.

Wild Flowers

Wild, that's what they call them
Wild, the colors a mix random
Wild, they dance in the wind
Wild, blown moving like waves
Wild, pleasant to the eye
Wild, light and aromatic
Wild, appealing to senses
Wild, they attract creatures
Wild, bees and bears
Wild, sheep and fawns
Wild, these flowers be

A Gull Imperched

Feathered and white headed
A gull scampers about the beach
Looking feverishly for opportunity
A morsel, a crust of bread perhaps
Left behind, the remnant
Of a picnic lunch
This futile search unsuccessful
To the air in a short flight
Following the avian activity
Not faraway
Upon joining the group
Hovering round a quarry unknown
All noise of chirps and caws
Breaks loose announcing
The invader who has alit
To crash the trove of chips
So closely guarded
These scavengers of the beach
Chase away this uninvited guest
Sending him to find a perch
To gaze only for
What come may.

Montauk Daisy

The blooming white and yellow
Where the black and orange monarchs
Come to rest while on their migration
Tell that summer's sweet time
Oh so mellow
Soon will be gone
The colors of autumn
Slowly replace your place upon the scene
Their vibrant shades
Created by the cold of October nights
With the November wind and rain
Like an impressionist's painting
Until shaken and blown
To the earth the leaves and flowers fall
Yet through it all
A reminder of summer's sun fun
Your smile remains
Til the first fallen snow

Chocolate

Chocolate, a gift of the God's
Heals the Stresses of the day
Oh, How sweet a
Candy for the spirit that
One at a time melts
Leaving that flavor which
Amazingly releases
Truly positive feelings all about me.
EXCELLENT!

Surf

Rolling in
Rolling out
Each time the same
Each time different
Tide is high
Tide is low
Breaking crashing down
Breaking pound, pound, pound
Sound of roar
Sound of power
Water gray
Water foaming
Always moving
Always coming
In and out
In and out
Ebb and flow
Ebb and flow

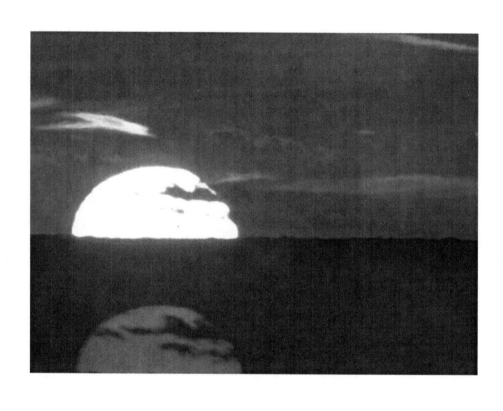

Sunrise

The air is cool as the darkness
Gradually gives way
To the first signs of light
Signaling the new day

The sand is soft
Accepting the imprint
Each step has left
Leaving a trail to follow
Til the next tide
Erases any trace of passing here

A breeze picks up
Coming in towards the shore
A quick shiver and then is gone
Warmed by the lightening skies
Revealing clouds kept
Secret by the night

With a burst of rays
The giant ball
Yellow big and hot
Out of the horizon
Rises against a sky
Now pumpkin orange
To take its place
Ever warming

Autumn

Cool crisp air of autumn
Trees changing color
The greens of spring and summer
Slowly becoming something softer
The chill slows the flow of green
Revealing a palette of earthy hues
Dazzling yellows, deep reds and browns
With many grays weaving in between
Changing each day
Growing brighter and more and more vivid . . .
Until the peak.

Slowly one by one
The colors fade
Browns and tans only
Leaves lose their grip upon the branches
Held tightly these many months
Floating gently, borne by wind
Spinning, almost dancing, on their journey
Finally coming to rest
Upon the ground.

Resting there the silence broken only
By the crunch when walked upon
Announcing someone's approach
Crunch, crunch, each step, like a mill
Reducing these once green shades of summers heat
Transformed, made leaf-meal
Ready to give up their elements
For the next generation
When the cycle of new growth resumes
In the spring

August

Sun warm in the sky
Wispy clouds seem to fly
Their shapes transform
Blown by currents
Passing unseen so high

An aroma of grass freshly mown
Fills the senses, feelings known
Warmth of the days
Cool of the nights
Joys of summer all our own

Gentle breeze from off the sea
Soft sound of surf rolling close to me
Wild flowers drawing butterflies
Gulls diving, geese flying
Summer stay, do not flee.

It is September

The sun sets a little earlier
Each day the air cools just a bit
Signaling the close of summer
The approach of autumn
The trees slowly start to change
Their deep green to reds and yellows
A few will fall to earth
Quietly landing but ready to crunch
Under the step of a passerby
It is September
Passed by is Labor's Day
Schools have opened
People try to remember
Tenderness in youth
And awe at the World Series
As cheers rise up from the gridiron
The crisp air is fitting for this time
Just as the season of harvest begins
This is your season
It is September

Moon Rise

The day slowly coming to a close
The waning red and purple of the western sky
Give way to the twilight blue
Of the fast approaching night
Rising up from the east
Over the horizon
A circle of light
A phantom of the mid day sun
Raises itself steadily
Reaching over the treetops
Giving a soft light
A light of shadows and dreams
To a world twinkling in reflection of itself
Almost as if on the other side of a looking glass
The moon softly rising
Full in its roundness
A perfect sphere
Floating as a sentinel above all
The air turned cool
A proper partner to this light of night
Relief from the hotness of day
Is changed and carries the evening sounds
A breeze rustling branches
An owl asking who goes there
Waits for a response
Responding is music
Floating across from the opposite shore
Giving a rhythm, a beat
To the song of the katydids
Til to moon goes to sleep
Welcoming the new morn

Morning Quiet

In the quiet of the pre-dawn light
All is still, motionless
A half dream silence
A silence not broken
Until the steadily rising illumination
A growing brightness
Caused by the eternal un-felt rotation
Leading us from the shadows of night
Awakens from the morning song bird
A song, soon en-chorused with many voices
Announcing the new day is here.

In half light half sleep
Half awake half raised up
From the silence of sleep
A morning song of our own
A prayer drawn out with a breath
Greets the day with praise
Thanks He Who is above all
Another chance given
To meet the marvels displayed
Before us in this world
This existence.

Spring

The day a little longer
Now the light lasts
All the way home
Following a sunset
Warm and yellow
Slowly giving way
For a warm orange hue
Which in turn itself
Gives up to the evening sky
Purple and blue
These are the first eves of spring
With crisp air most pleasant
Fresh with the aroma of a thousand budding trees
Paired with the scent of daffodils
While the forsythia erupts in yellow
Their branches now perches
Upon which robins a swallows rest
Waiting to dive upon the next seed they see
Happy days of spring are here.

Surety

The sun rises o'er the horizon
A giant ball
Shining light on the world
Making colors
Come alive
With the coming of the day
Comes time again
To fall in love with you
My soul-mate, my muse
To whom I say I do
Ten thousand times
Or more
What joy to experience
Each time the sun rises and sets
The tides ebb and flow
Love by God's unending hand
Fills my open soul.

A Beautiful Day

A beautiful day
How many of these
Have I seen now
Since I first saw day
Knowing not what bright is
Knowing that it is, wondering?
Being in the moment
So many of these days
Too many to count
Why count them
For each is as different as the next
Etched in my memory
Each unique
This day the numbered years match
Only one of six times to see this
Signals perhaps a new age
No longer a child
Still a wife, a mother
Still a caring professional
Yes perhaps a new age
Still now I see the bright
I know what it is and wonder at it beauty
I say thanks
I say yes!

May Day

Oh! How sweet
The smell
Of the clean spring air.
The scent of tulips
Pansies and forsythia
Is intoxicating,
Like the bouquet of
New spring wine.
Oh so filling
To my senses,
The rising sunlight
Shimmers on the morning dew
Making a thousand tiny rainbows dance
On top of the blades of new mown grass.
Oh how beautiful,
Oh how great,
Oh how wonderful,
This day, oh this day
So like the one, now many years past,
My lover, my lady, my joy
Entered my life
Changing it forever.
She is all the sweetness of springtime,
The sweetness of the new blooms;
The aroma of new life she is.
Her kisses so sweet,
Sweeter than wine,
Awe me.

Fun at the Beach

It is a cold December day
Too cold to go swimming
The trees are bare
Sea grass now straw colored
Ice forms on the sand
Salt forms on the drying rocks
The cold goes to the bone.
I like to think of warmer climes
Sun and warmth filling days
Love and more love the nights
Walking barefoot in the sand
Leaving footprints the next wave erases
Waves gently breaking
Like a clock marking time
Sounds of laughter, children playing
Birds calling each other announcing a feast
Picnickers have come
A pleasant memory for this winter day
My mind pondering backward to reach
Fun at the beach.

Love

A Man, A Woman

A man, a woman, lovers
Like love birds stop to hover
Mid field of tall wild grasses
Mixed with wild flowers passes
A butterfly who alights nearby
A soaring bird in the sky
Colorful with sweet smell
The only witnesses to tell
Peaceful to rest in
Like a new found Eden

A man, a woman, lovers
Each tuned in discovers
Sight, taste, smell
A trust known well
Sparkles like a sunlit raindrop
Silent time seems to stop
Here to be to laze
Touch, feel, amaze
All senses shutter and abound
Within these moments found

A man, a woman, lovers
No words to utter
Bubbling like a stream
Passion so filled with steam
Ignites under sunny cloudless skies
Until finished to simply lie
Motionless entwined
As one divined
Paused in loving embrace
Heart strings do vibrate
A song and all about flutters
A man, a woman, lovers

A Way I Love You

Oh my! Myself I love you as I do
How or why not knowing
Just doing as if designed before time
By instinct
Loving in the now, the present
Being in the moment
Every inhaled breath
Takes in that which is you
The aroma of your essence
An aura so sweet
Excites every inch of my being
With each touch comes a tingling
Leading ever forward
Holding you close
A kiss, an embrace
Body pressing against body
Passion rising to its zenith level
Synchronized one heart one love together
A duet a way born to be
A being in purpose
United with you my lover
My mistress, my muse
How you do inspire me.

Acknowledgement

For so long now
Often silent
Yet ever knowing
Assured with confidence
Buoyed with a love unconditional
Acknowledgement is due
Support from you
Faithful, strong and true
A trusted guide leading
Through situations sometimes strained
Like a weight hanging
From a frayed cord
Pain and sadness
Remediated, made bearable
Knowing you are near
Holding me up
As a buttress hold a wall
So it will not crumble
Fall or heap itself
Into a pile, unrecognizable
Rubble, debris, a mess
My angel, my guide, my dear
Words inadequately express thanks
For from you this is given
Hope in the silver lining
The sun that shines behind the clouds
With rays that chase darkness away
Gently saying it will be alright.

Beyond Rubies

Beyond all riches is she
My Lover, My wife.
A gift beyond compare with any in life
For earthly values here know not her spirit
Or detect the gentleness of heart to hear it.
A character so noble
Inspires me to hold too
Tenderness of virtue
Impossible to measure or weigh
Loving and passionate at play
Patient under duress
Smiling and forgiving weaknesses
Healing from here to there
Gracious with tender care.
Humbly frustrations put aside
Comforting wiping tears from eyes
Reddened from weakness of spirit
Listening an ability of merit
With words of life so true
Saying "it's alright, I love you"
Erasing all signs of strife
My lover, my wife
Beyond all riches is she.

Curves

Curves, so many curves
Connected, not one straight line among them
Together molded in just the right way
Reveal your image.

Like clay in a sculptors' hands
Gently kneaded, gently massaged
Placed side by side
This image appears.

The curve of a brow
Just above ellipses of eyes
Windows, the entry to the soul
Hover just above the essence of lips
Sloping softly upward in a smile
All framed in an oval face
A face that makes my defenses melt.

Absorbed into these curves,
Curves of passion and love
My hand touches them and soars over
Like a bird in the sky
Its soft feathers caressing the air
The air on which it glides effortlessly
Until it alights upon a happy place
A place of curves . . . you.

Sense and Listen

When I listen to you
All of my senses
Are put to work
It is simply
Not sufficient
Just to hear
More than that
I need to feel
Taste and see
To appreciate
The deep innermost person
My lover
Revealing herself to me

I listen patiently
Anticipating
Every delicious word
Words with an aroma
Understood only
By a lover who has beheld them
In the deep embrace of passion
They fill my senses
Overwhelming at times
My very ability to comprehend
Their meaning
Saving by the grace of love
Through which they are given.

To Be Enjoy!

Enjoy in Marriage
Brings with it the image
Many things coming to focus
Which lie within the hearts of us
Time spent in close contact
Dramas played . . . each by act
Roads travelled side by side
Never in time has been such a ride
Adventure with all it brings
Makes my very being sing
About the beauty 'round us shared
Hand in hand we two paired
Together on this road of life
You, me, husband and wife
Lovers joined in passion
Shared intensely like on a mission
Like an electric attraction I feel charged

Powering a dynamo . . . our love grown large
Like a rainbow spanning the sky
Fireworks burst while we fly by
Into our arms
Where none can harm
Gently we lie to rest
Doing what we love best
Free to be who we are
Such a great asset by far
Filled with love divine
Faith tells all is fine
More than all money
You are the best gift my honey
Being married to you
Only my "yes" can ensue
Every moment with you I must employ
A shout from me which says . . . I ENJOY!

Watery Eyes

My eyes water in joy
To be so honored
Experiencing the love
Given by you, my lover and friend
Received by me and given again
Exchanged from those deep places
Our hearts save for us alone
To embrace that which is our
Special state
Unity Joy Love

Open Hands

With open hands
I try to grab each syllable
As they pass the lips
So many times I have kissed
Again and again kissed
Capturing each sound
To take on their energy
The energy of Love
Gazing into those blue eyes
Eyes so beautiful and soft
I see the source of the love,
Love which formed feelings
Feelings held deep, deep within.
This most wondrous souls'
Gift of feelings
Gift of self
So profound, so magnificent
Humbles me
Making me realize
I must bow to its greatness and
With every part of me
Listen.

The Pen

Across the page
The pen moves
Letters flowing out
From the tip
Putting down in words
Those intangible things
We call feelings.

Ink upon paper
Black upon white
Bordered between
Lines of blue
Framed as it were
Making a picture with words
What you mean to me.

These words describe
As best they can
The real me
I that am
Vulnerable, at risk
And in love
Totally, completely with you.

Laughter

When to the fore comes a certain path
On a journey which brings me closer
To the one with whom I would join
In an embrace, which when it was finished
Leaves me exhausted,
I will follow it with joyful expectation.

That embrace . . . holding arms
So lithe as branches in springtime
Full of the sweet aroma of newly opened blossoms
Penetrates the deepest regions of my being
Comes to rest in the center of my heart.

Moving like leaves
Pushed on by the wind
The cares and adornments
Carried during the day, float
And gently fall
Not making a sound for nothing
Could interrupt the concentration
Of each upon the focus of the other.

The warm touching
Of such deep emotion
Makes it impossible not to lose one's being,
As each is consumed by the other
Into something new.
Pulsating, the heart beats faster and faster,
Emotion more and more intense
Rising higher and higher still
Until leaping out, at that supreme moment
When one is truly free to release the true self,
From the voice comes . . . Laughter.

Our Dialogue

Our Dialogue is . . .
A journey
Through a land of discovery
Every word and feeling conveyed
Like upon the turning of a corner
Losing one's breath gazing at the new vista!

Our dialogue is . . .
The luscious sweet taste of berries
Picked ripe in springtime
Complimented by a full-bodied wine
Dark and woody
Finished off with a flourish of dark chocolate!

Our dialogue is . . .
A gentle rocking
Like when seated on the foredeck of a sloop
Quietly running on a gentle sea
Just as the dawn breaks upon the horizon
Filling the sky with wondrous orange-yellow light
Warming the body and soul!

Our dialogue is . . .
Sensitivity
The kind that goes off the scale
Like the warm embrace of a passionate kiss
Long-lasting and patient
That fills the body and senses
With a pleasure only true lovers know!
Our dialogue is . . .

Mother's Day

Carried for so long
Listening to the steady beat
Thump, thump, thump,
A sound that was safe, secure, reassuring
A bond both physical and emotional,
Unbreaking,
Forged to last, though eventually severed,
Remains a bond eternal.
Once emerged,
Still called back by that sound
Smell and touch added
Safe again
Fed, nourished and loved
Loved in the best way capable
So much given up
So much sacrificed
So much wanted
Given up so others might spread their wings
Always what needed
Supplied
Taught to listen
Taught to love
How many selfless acts . . .
Too many to count
Love . . . love only a mother gives
Love . . . only a mother is

When First I Loved You

When First I loved you,
My heart floated above the ground
Soaring in the vastness of blue
Like an eagle in flight not making a sound
Taking in your radiant beauty
Knowing nothing will ever be the same
To you I will surrender the key
To unlock my heart so we two are twain
No longer to journey the world alone
To face ahead what not can tell
To be with you wherever, is home
In you I have found my angel.

Waiting

Oh my dear lady
I am anxious
So anxious
With anticipation I await
Await with an intensity
Too great to measure
Waiting
Waiting for your return

Lying awake in the deep night
Before the light of dawn
Starts to creep through the glass
Missing the soothing sound of
Each breath you draw
Missing the touch of you
Lying beside me
Clutching your pillow
I am restless
Waiting
Waiting for your return.

Stumbling around
Roaming about
Aimless
Eating without tasting
Watching without seeing
Speaking without talking
Just lost in thought
Waiting
Waiting for your return.

I am here
But not here
My spirit travels the distance
The space between us
Longing to be with you
Whispering I love you
Softly in your ear.
Yet my body,
This physical form,
Remains yet here
Trapped in space and time
Waiting
Waiting for your return.

bide

My dear
Abide with me awhile
Take some time
Step back from the pile
All will be fine

Away from work and worry
Sit and rest
No need to scurry
You can have the best

Let your heart be open
With love and desire
It will soon happen
We'll be afire

What will it fashion
Together we will see
Love and passion
My dear
Abide with me.

Sixty Four

Sixty-four is a sizable number:
'Tis the sum of the first eight odds.
How can one measure time?
In a period of sixty-four years
There is an illusion, a conundrum, a paradox,
Of standing still yet moving if at all
Slower than a turtle pulling itself along
But looking up and seeing time has passed
In an instant filled with so much life.

Sixty-four a number beautiful filled with life
Not yet complete says the I Ching
Imaged by fire and water
Important element but also symbols
Symbols of the choices
Drawing us closer to the source of ultimate Love
That Love which brings peace, fulfillment and serenity.

Sixty-four the route, Serenity the goal
The destination only reached
After passing through time and space
A place where one discovers the self
The skin in which one is happy to stay
Content in the moment where one is.

Sixty-four is not measured
Like a set of days, sun up to sundown
More like a circle of color
Coming from the darkness opening to
Reds, oranges yellows and blues
Before returning to the violets and reds
It is a colorful parade of life
A kaleidoscope always moving
Turning and changing shape.

Sixty-four, the not completed
Leads us to hope
Hope, the colors, the love, the serenity, continue
The understanding that time
While moving ever forward
Slowly uncovers more beauty
More wonder, more excitement
Making it clear to us that
The sum of sixty-four is ten.

Next to You

My favorite place
In the world
Is next to you.
Anywhere
Any time
Any place
The cold white north
The lush green tropics
By the shore
Counting the rhythm
Waves breaking on shore
Colors in the sunset
Beautiful when
Reflected on you
Warm my spirit
Even if cold
Aside a fire
Warming each other
Softly set against
Nighttime air
A hug
A long, long kiss
Another hug
My favorite place
In the world
Is next to you.

Patience

Patience
Virtue of virtues
A cardinal one for sure
For time can stretch
It's call to sufferance
With those laborious trials
That brings us to abuse

Patience
To be able to wear
Like a jacket, protection
From the restlessness tethered
To us demanding equanimity
Seeking only to abide
With the quibbling
Around us

Patience
Time consuming, it tempers
Ground in a crucible
A resignation exasperated
Like a Stylite's perseverance
To a trespass tribulation
Waiting to pounce
Devouring nerve

Patience
A gift of the Spirit
That fills with longanimity
My cheesed off attitude
And like Penelope
Saintly abiding
Can bear beyond
The saturation point.

Feelings, Vaules and Emotions

There are feelings, values and emotions;
held deep within the complex areas;
areas that surrounds the mind and the heart.
So many being held there,
the line between them becomes blurred;
each obscuring the other.
Do they belong to the heart,
or should they be exiled to the head,
and thereby placed in one box or another,
along with all my thoughts.
These feelings . . . so many . . . so many,
each with its specific description which to it belong.
These feelings . . . so varied . . . so opposite,
yet existing, side by side as it were,
bonded to each other by one unifying factor,
right or wrong they are not . . . they just are.
Why does it take so long to realize,
what we value is part of us?
Feelings and emotions, these are the players
who describe who we are.
Is this why we protect them so dearly,
keeping them inside where it is safe,
for they are us?
They are me.

The Kiss

Like a moment
Caught in time
These lovers gently embracing
Arms entwined
Lips together
As one.

How often
My love
I have held your softness
Like this
Cannot be counted
As one

Like numbering
The stars
Or grains of sand
By the sea
Love runs over
From two
As one

Overflowing a cup
Graces poured out
Refreshing. blessing
Our spirits in unity
Forever, always we
As one.

A Way Unimaginable

I love you in a way unimaginable
This love runs so deep within my spirit
That looking down in a valley
Green, verdant, full of color
With a stream of life giving water
Flowing through it
When followed seeing it meet the sea
With all its extreme of depths
Approaches how deep
The vision is
My love for you

I love you in a way unimaginable
The aroma of you, a scent, an essence
Excites my spirit
Drawing within
A desire to empty
All of me into you
To gaze into that essence
Your eyes like a clear summer sky
Raises me to float like an eagle
Supported by air, a cushion
Gently keeping me aloft.

I love you in a way unimaginable
In my youth I would consume
Older I am consumed
In the specter of your embrace
It is here the true meaning
Oneness, the joining of souls
Touching each other
In passion
Rifts the constraint of space-time
Dimensions no longer boxing in
The gift of self blooms
Like a garden
Filled with overpowering sweetness
I love you . . .

The Empty Page

I am so plain
Lifeless
Not a trace
Or any mark
Of pen, pencil or ink
Out of my emptiness
I beckon
Come. fill me.

I am like a glass
Waiting to hold a libation
Refreshment, not liquid
But of lines and curves
Letters formed quenching
The readers thirst
For understanding
Love and affirmation
I beckon
Come, fill me.

I am blank
A void to be transformed
Animated, given life
By words yet unformed
A hot pen depositing feelings
Felling of love, desire and emotion
Shaping a picture
An image of self
In words risked for a lovers trust.
I beckon
Come, fill me.

Naked

Naked bare
Two persons standing
The state au-naturel
Not the peachy stuff
Sophomoronic youth ogle over
Like a streaker
Aimlessly strutting skinship
Adrift at sea in a false
Self-abasing nudism
Naked bare

Naked bare
No a different visual
For the first time exposed
Like a new flower
Excited as under a spell
This perception close held
A binary vision known only
By lovers in confidence
Naked bare

Naked bare
This nudity of feelings
Escaping each other like
Rays of light from a singularity
Free of the gravity that held them
Allowing the other to see
The individual each is
Like the day born
No shame, undressed
Defenseless safe
Naked bare

A Valentine for Regina

Accept my dear, the words here written,
Between the lines lie feelings sown within
Feelings so very often we each seek
To which we ourselves to each other alone will speak.
Sometimes so we may be weary
In the sharing we often make merry
Never taken such in jest
Our love is genuine expressed
Oh you are still the image so sweet and slender
Visions flash before me of actions tender
Your blue eyes so brightly shine
In love I seek you my Valentine
Oh how time seems so fleeting
'Tis like yesterday our meeting
Since each other we took as own
I still say I love you alone.
So take these words and keep them near
Their meaning must be completely near
Be sure as the sun does shine
Always you are my Valentine

Photo Index

Cover Photo: Twin Falls, Tracy's Arm, AK
Author Photo: Taken near LaCompte Glacier, AK

CPSIA information can be obtained at www.ICGtesting.com
Printed in the USA
BVOW040400281212

309275BV00003B/241/P